Aurélienne Dauguet

Activate your inner healer

MERANO VERLAG

Cover design:
A big thank you to Claudia Zanvit for the special photo on the book cover: enso2@mac.com

Bibliographic information from the German National Library: The German National Library lists this publication in the Deutsche Nationalbibliografie; detailed bibliographic data can be accessed on the Internet at http://dnb.dnb.de.

Bibliografische Information der Deutschen Nationalbibliothek:

Die Deutsche Nationalbibliothek verzeichnet diese Publikation in der Deutschen Nationalbibliografie; detaillierte bibliografische Daten sind im Internet über http://dnb.dnb.de abrufbar.

Herstellung: BoD - Books on Demand, Norderstedt

ISBN: 978-3-944700-74-8 (Paperback)

ISBN: 978-3-944700-84-7 (e-book)

Table of contents

PART 1: MULTIDIMENSIONALITY OF BEING AND ITS DIFFERENT APPROACHES

Communication with the different levels of self
trust instead of drama
The regenerative powers of the organism

You as a living human being are multidimensional. You are versatile in the nature of your being and you have numerous different aspects. Some are part of your conscious self: your kind facet, your angry part, your weird habits, your cosmic striving, your aching knee, your mindfulness and/or sloppiness tendencies, your submissive tendencies, and your dominating tendencies. And much more.

You have evolved and nurtured multiple levels of your existence up until now. You are the multifaceted expression of your unity. Comparable to the disco ball with its countless facets, you radiate out into the world. How you are, how you think you are, how you would like to be and how you should be: numerous aspects of the one inside that are in constant flux.

How do you deal with all this, with the changing roles: mother, wife, writer, buyer, therapist, sister, aunt, neighbor, recipient, giver, clarifier, tax slave, activist, sleepyhead and more...

EXERCISE A:

Here is an important visualization to internalize your versatility: All facets of the mirror ball are connected to a highly concentrated point in the center. The more of those converge into the central focus of the sphere, the more stable your being is. From this core you can interact calmly and confidently with your many aspects. This center in you gives you the necessary overview as well as a concentration of energy that enables a balanced mediation and interaction between the parts of your being.

It is your goal to approach this shining, golden point in the middle of your personal universe and aim at it as a lighthouse. This point of light is your essence: it is the unity within you that is expressed outwardly as diverse aspects of your personality. That point of light that you have forgotten, that distracts you but constantly reminds you. Please listen!

Few are aware that their invisible part is infinitely greater than their visible part.

The eternal part that has not incarnated gives life to the visible and ephemeral, i.e., the will to live, liveliness and vitality. It is not enough just to live, but vitality must be maintained through strength and will. Everything is constantly on - going process , a process in transition.

This light of life in the center of your sphere (your universe) plays an essential role in your task as an inner healer. It is accessible through your thinking/feeling in the form of a conscious and unconscious exchange. It can be reached and influenced by electrical impulses from the neurovegetative system and by hormonal - chemical messages. It is worth going inside and starting from there again and again to determine where you are and to ask yourself: How do I feel in my body, in my emotional world, in my being? And then you turn to the current state of your personality to question it in the same way. In this context, I differentiate between feeling and emotion. The emotion conveys its subjective and specific message, the feeling is immediate and does not lie. The head sometimes tells stories - or what you would like to hear. However, when head and heart are in sync, we receive a reliable response that can guide and even save our health, situation, or life. From this special head - heart constellation we get the inspiration, the unshakable knowledge, the flash of inspiration together with the deepest insights. Specifically, while placing our hand on the heart chakra in the center of our chest, we ponder the desired topic.

You may know your inner child, your inner woman, or your vulnerable part, your brave role. Likewise, one of your most important aspects is arguably your inner healer.

Just as everyone has an inner child - because we were all children - we have a healer part, since we all, without exception, have enormous self-healing powers. These keep us alive and promote our everyday regeneration processes, both small and large.

EXERCISE B:

Please pause to give gratitude to this precious, natural capacity for self-healing within you. Choose a quiet moment, sit down and turn your gaze inward, perhaps at an event or affliction from which you have partially or fully recovered. Feel gratitude, relief, and satisfaction that the problem, discomfort, is over. "Thank you that I'm fine, better, better and better!" Really feel into it: the relaxation, the detachment, the liberation and at the same time the strengthening that arose from the healing or the solution. Feel that deep in your being: what a relief! What a miracle! "How grateful I am that my being, my body, has recovered from this hurdle/disease!" Yes, say it. Let the tears flow, in case they want to come up: tears of appreciation, tears of joy, of connection that you direct to your own healing powers. Visualize your healthy, balanced state. Feeling good is a blessing and a sign that balance has been restored. The fact that you are experiencing and expressing gratitude intensifies the whole experience of (again) being whole.

By no means do I use the term healing in a medical sense, but I refer to the natural rhythm of regeneration in the flow of the original life force. It creates and creates, repairs and redesigns again and again in accordance with the present order of the living power of the ether, the elements and the light (prana or orgone and other names for the elemental power in action). This means that the powers of renewal are constantly at work and continuously adapt to the respective demands of the organism. The condition for this is that there must be more life force than the daily maintenance requires. The more "excess" life force, the stronger the immune system and the regenerative abilities of the physical body.

This inner healer (I will use both variants alternately) as she/he suits us. You can visualize her/him, give her/him a name and other characteristics. There is no limit to creativity and imagination to bring this healing, caring entity to mind. The more concretely and closely their presence is experienced, the more effective their harmonizing activity. However, the most important thing is trust in your own healing presence: confidence in your abilities, in your immediate help, in your differentiation and reliability. As in any relationship of trust, an advance of trust is necessary at the beginning or at least the openness to deal with it. Over time, however, the feedback from the body will empirically prove its effectiveness. As you collect more positive results, trust grows exponentially. These are the miracles of the inner healer. They can accompany us until our last breath. The relationship between the person and their inner healer works better when it is characterized by respect, gratitude and flexibility.

This does not preclude us from receiving advice and collecting and processing data. On the contrary - it is important to obtain detailed information and to let one's own ability to differentiate prevail. However, the final decision is made intuitively with and by the healing part. Time, consistency and a clear and precise diary-keeping are essential to deal with information, observations, impressions and the inner healing authority in a more differentiated way. The benefits are to be appreciated: independence, self-responsibility, and tailored healing impulses that resonate with your inner integrity. In addition, the inner healer is always present. It may warn you in advance with prophylactic insights and bodily reactions and messages through synchronicities or mental intuitions - if you are receptive and mindful.

EXERCISE C:

Take some time right away to develop a relationship with your spiritual guide. The interaction promotes self-knowledge, depth and autonomy. When she's stable and resting on a confident, clear expectation, all goes smoothly and free of drama. For the simple reason that the body, its language and the feedback from the healer are coordinated: access to it is individual and therefore as unique as every human being. It is best to choose a level of discomfort to practice as an opportunity to connect with your inner helper and establish free communication with it. For example, by asking questions such as "What would do you good: rest, gentle activity or vigorous exercise? warmth or coolness?"

"What food do my cells need?" Do small, simple experiments that show a direct effect. This practice reduces the alienation between you, your physical aspect and your wisdom. Pay attention and talk to him: because everything in the universe is exchange, energy flow and transmission of life force and resonance. The simpler and clearer the communication, the simpler and clearer the answer from your subconscious.

In the next sections we want to address the different levels: body, sensation and emotion, mental cinema and intellect, the inner divine and the energetic.

Here I would like Dr. To paraphrase Albert Schweizer: "I'll tell you that we doctors actually do very little. We only send an impulse to the organism so that it heals itself. We don't heal."

PART 2 : THE BODY

The body as ally, vehicle, temple of the soul and stepping
stone to the plane of manifestation.
dealing with discomfort
Shifts / changes
Resistance forces and regulatory therapy
Pain is his emergency language: Please listen first!
Movement and its advantages according to Dr. Wendy Suzuki

Most people identify with their body and its shape, height,
weight and other visible characteristics. Not only is this sense
of self limited, but it affects the ephemeral, mortal aspect.
Which represents a tremendous obstacle to the development
of the soul. This view reduces our eternal essence to a
temporary existence unrelated to origin and fulfillment of soul
purpose. No wonder most lack genuine self-esteem, self-
respect, and self-acceptance, which affects many human
relationships.

Dealing with the body is ambivalent or contradictory in many
cultures, whether western or eastern: from body cult in the
material world to the suppression of physicality. In the first
version only the appearance, the weight, the mechanics and
the measuring of the material part count. The eternal cult of
beauty and youth as well as intrusive medicine are his altar.
Immortality of the body is sought (frozen or as clones) to
compensate for ignorance of the immortality of the soul's

consciousness. As a result - and somehow in a contradictory way - his passing represents a final farewell - with all the fears, despair and insecurities that go with it. Man is then "gone forever", victim of his fate, without meaning or purpose. In the second version, the body is gross, seductive, and painful—associated with sin and suffering. Many people are afraid of their body: that it will do "unpredictable" things (allergies, skin reactions, changes in blood pressure, pain, inflammation, weight gain or loss, etc.). The term "unpredictable" includes a "surprise effect", a feeling of being at the mercy and finally a touch of "hostility": "What is it doing again? Why does it hurt It just has to stop! I just want to get rid of the discomfort." In doing so, he constantly sent information and gradually made his message clearer and clearer until pain arises: and then it is finally noticed... - but maybe not taken that seriously - or is it? Please listen to what he has to say!

And so there is fear and confusion in the closest relationship there is, between the soul and the body in which it resides during incarnation.

The physical aspect is "the vehicle" whereby the soul finds expression on earth in human - or animal and vegetable - form. In the material world, the eternal aspect requires an ephemeral, physical portion in order to materialize. From the information of the previous incarnation, he is endowed with certain qualities that are necessary and meaningful for this life. Physicality is the basic condition of our existence here.

The soul rests in the body: the material part is the vessel or temple of the soul. From that perspective alone, there should always be gratitude for this physical appearance, and mindfulness, and also joy and admiration for the miracles it is doing. The body is the interface between the subtle and gross dimensions. Not only is it necessary to the experience we are having on planet Earth, but its state (whether healthy, fit, energetic, debilitated, or ill) directly affects the quality of the experiences we attract and accumulate. A few examples that impair or increase the state of mind: When we are hungry, we lack mental and spiritual concentration and we cannot meditate. When we suffer from constipation we feel uncomfortable, tired, heavy, blocked. When we are seriously ill, our overall quality of life is significantly affected. They are two different versions of the same person having different experiences, whether ailing or fit and buoyant.

EXERCISE A:

Become aware of how your physical state influences your perception of events, your enjoyment and appreciation of life and even your intellectual reflections. Please emphasize the difference with concrete examples: in the state of healthy well-being - but also when the body feels discomfort. Thank your physical body for the different tasks it handles and accomplishes. Please don't just say "thank you", but really feel the gratitude down to the cells: the grateful vibration should reach there!

This is a nice exercise for beginners. It is also always suitable for making contact with the intelligence of the body. This intelligence is not only nourished but stimulated by the attention it deserves. Have fun and above all: a nice connection to your material vehicle!

Even if the body is not comfortable, you can develop an excellent relationship with it. Instead of feeling fear, shame, or helplessness, meet him with interest and curiosity: touch him gently and lovingly. look at him Talk to him. Start an intimate relationship with him. The big advantage is that you deal with him honestly and authentically. He knows everything about you anyway. He goes along with everything. You can address specific parts of the body and ask why they are now manifesting this discomfort and what could be the causes behind it.

Your focus, your voice, your interest and possibly your touch (the laying on of your hand) will make the body region behave differently. She may relax and become receptive to healing impulses and higher vibrations. The opening immediately relieves tension and pressure, promotes blood circulation and starts the process of regeneration. The cells are intelligent and telepathic, registering mindful intent immediately. This reaction may be very noticeable or barely noticeable, depending on how sensitive the observer is and how healthy or unhealthy the spot is. But an energetic approach certainly exists, as confirmed by quantum physics. The observer influences the observed. Negative feelings directed at the body are absorbed by the tissue as energy draining and frequency reducing. A careful observation of the area with the intention of understanding why it feels painful, swollen, congested is positively received: the vibration immediately rises and sets an impulse towards improvement. Most of the time the reaction will be minimal the 1st time. But sometimes it is really noticeable. Sometimes the mindful handling works like a miracle and supports and intensifies every kind of treatment. And every situation is unique and a very special encounter with your body!

Observing that a shift is taking place is confirmation that an interaction is present. Congestion is pathological, painful, entropic. Energy movement is evidence that decongestion is taking place. Life is flux and movement and eddying, as Schauberger, the great explorer, demonstrated about water and the essence of life. From an energetic point of view, the goal is to send an impulse and thereby promote vitality. A little push can make a big difference. Less is more. Let wise nature find its course again. Observe and accompany the process without activism. Nature constantly seeks balance, healing, well-being. Create the right environment for this by resting, listening and observing. The polarity throws the state of balance out of harmony again and again and gives it the opportunity to come back into line with the blueprint. In it lies the frequency of health, of balance, and it will mobilize everything to get back on track. The knowledge rests in the DNA, in the cells, in the morphic field but also in the aura.

It makes sense to deal with the individual characteristics of your physical body. As in any relationship, it makes sense to visualize who we are dealing with, how we want to communicate and what we would like to experience together. I have reported extensively on the physical body in my book SETTING HEALTHY BOUNDARIES. He needs time to integrate new information in order to implement the change in the cells and in the tissue. It works slower than the ghost. But it is very receptive to healthy impulses. Unfortunately, he is just as susceptible to doubt or self-deprecation. It has its own pace and is a little different every day. Consideration, respect and mindfulness are a good strategy when communicating with him, as well as patient progress in everyday processes.

You see: the way you deal with your cells is comparable to the interaction with your fellow human beings. In the initial stages, it is advisable to be careful. When we know each other better, we may be able to trust ourselves more, and yet we should always be mindful. You feel a deep connection with your ally, so you can anticipate their reaction and gauge their limits.

The body gives us feedback through its physical signs. They show either an improvement, a deterioration or a constant condition. If we limit ourselves to a black and white assessment, we may come to invalid conclusions. Positive is not just an improvement, but possibly a change that progresses from chronic to acute discomfort. There is a brief initial aggravation that in itself creates a healthy shift. Where the traffic jam clears, the river begins to move, sometimes accompanied by acute uneasiness. Imagine this blocked energy that has accumulated over the years. The healing impulse sets it in motion. In a nutshell, this is a simple but apt description of the healing process from chronic blockages. Chronic must first become acute in order to be cured in order for it to make its way out of the body.

The pain is a message from the body to draw attention to a disharmony. The child cries to express suffering and to focus on their needs. The discomfort is an expression of the body to convey that something is out of balance. Please listen to this message, take it seriously instead of repressing it or trying to numb it. The pain is a cry for help. The healing attention can work wonders: it can lead us to modify habits and behaviors e.g., our diet. This can result in a leap in consciousness. The therapeutic focus wants to understand the workings of the body so that it can provide what is needed. At a higher level, directing the healing intent toward the ailment or disharmony imparts a nurturing and "ordering" impulse to the tissues that are out of balance. Directing recognition and acceptance to the spot has a healing effect in the original sense of "one again, whole again / holy / or make perfect". When the child, the human being, the animal, the plant and all living things are bathed in mindfulness, the aliveness of the being rises. His aura expands. The vibration increases and allows the original order to be restored.

That's why dr. Bircher-Benner, other doctors and healers (e.g. Pastor Sebastian Kneipp) called their healing method order therapy. These basic supportive measures are non-invasive and adapt to the body's basic needs. Their synergetic effect is rarely absent. They can also be successfully incorporated in parallel or in addition to other treatments.

Physical activity and the joy of exercise not only have a positive effect on your physical condition, but also on your psychological and mental health. The neuroscientist Dr. Wendy A. Suzuki has conducted personal and laboratory research into the restorative effects of exercise on mood and memory. In addition, it has been shown that regular exercise has a preventive effect against neurodegenerative diseases such as Parkinson's or Alzheimer's. Personally, I have experienced the regenerative function of physical challenge during my transition to light feeding. It became even more impressive as I moved more and more: I found that I get strength or a kind of nourishment and satiation directly from the joy of movement. Physical activity became a source of energy and nourishment for me. This is in stark contrast to what I had learned, which is that exercise makes you tired and hungry. In addition, I have observed that sport is conducive to intellectual activity. After that, the brain is well supplied with blood, loaded with fresh oxygen and stimulated. In addition, through the discipline of the body, eager and new synapses are formed. I wish you a lot of fun with your physical mobility! The important thing is that you find the right level and type of activity for you and also update it regularly to match your current needs.

The better we know our own body, the more it becomes our ally. We gain greater self-control as he becomes more responsive to subtle vibrations and spiritual insights. We then become our own experts, self-experts. We recognize quiet messages and can remedy deficiencies early on, compensate for too much or too little or discard unfavorable habits. Being able to trust your body is a blessing. Working together with him, learning from him and enjoying this naturally healthy life with him into old age are reserved for people who work on themselves. It's worth it. Unfortunately, the majority behave as if their body is a disposable item. You let yourself be stunned when it's time to start the big journey: the crossing over, for which we actually need enlightening clarity. The "knowing" physical body guides us through the various steps instead of being paralyzed by fear of death. What dimensions do you think you will land in when your awareness is clouded and distorted by fear, drugs, and ignorance. Probably not in the highest spiritual dimensions. Ideally, the body will act as an ally as it begins to prepare for the Great Letting Go. Those who are receptive and clear in spirit and in tune with their soul are able to receive and accept the message. Even if saying goodbye as a person is not necessarily easy for him. In any case, he will not fight back in fear and terror.

Let me introduce a quote from Wolfgang von Goethe on the perceptual apparatus of the human body as receiver and transmitter: "Humans themselves, insofar as they use their healthy senses, are themselves the largest and most precise physical apparatus that can exist. And the greatest misfortune of the new physics is that the experiments have been separated from human beings, so to speak, and nature is only to be recognized with what artificial instruments show, indeed what it can achieve, thereby limiting and proving it. Through the aura, the nadis and the chakras, through the meridian system and through the lesser-known skin plaque, which have been studied and documented by the Italian psychiatrist Giuseppe Calligaris (1876-1944). In the 30s and 40s of the last century he used his method - called Psiram - to apply pressure to certain areas of the skin and linked it to precise paranormal abilities. His work must be quite valuable given the CIA's curiosity about it and Wikilie 's scathing articles on his research.

EXERCISE B:

A simple exercise, but one that takes a little time to master, is finding out the foods that your body needs. What happens when you ditch that drink, those fries, and permanently replace them with something else? Food can affect the body and its performance, as well as its mental and intellectual abilities such as concentration, alertness and even the formation of synapses. Dumbing down begins with food, the news completes it. It is worth doing something to develop our basic skills and to be able to represent true human dignity as human beings.

This exercise may turn into an individually designed know-how that saves your health and improves your life in the long term. At the same time you can develop an excellent intuition that you can implement for pragmatic applications. Your own physicality with its countless "antennas" gives you constant, infallible feedback.

Now I would like to address the physical body as a stepping stone to the plane of manifestation. Physicality is the condition for experiencing reality, but also for materially shaping our lives. With our hands we "make" and gain power or power over matter, objects and events around us. The body is essential for the implementation of thoughts, ideals, visions in the world of manifestation. This includes physical strength and endurance but also special talents, skills and creativity. It functions as the gross expression of the soul, for which it is also necessary to have the human experience on earth and in the body.

In short, a healthy and agile body is not only able to create many things, but also to experience and enjoy beautiful things. The creative flow of energy winds through material reality, where it expresses the deep aspirations of vision.

CONCLUSION: Your physical body is your best friend. It makes your experience on earth not only possible, but enjoyable, rich, experiential. The healthier it is, the freer and more flowing are the experiences you make. It's up to you to find out what he likes, what's good for him, what his rhythms and priorities are. He is completely unique. It is therefore your responsibility to get to know it and to care for it in such a simple, natural and mindful manner. For this he is in constant dialogue with you and gives you feedback: Please listen to him! You are your own expert!

PART 3 : SENSATION AND EMOTION

Observe, name, acknowledge, confront
Increase frequency and transform energy.
Feedback: Satisfied feedback as a sign of spiritual harmony.

I have described the emotional body in detail in my book SETTING HEALTHY BOUNDARIES. He is changeable, sometimes likes drama and transmits his conditions directly to the physical body: high blood pressure, facial flushing, impotence and frigidity, dumbness, hyperactivity or torpor, and other physiological reactions.

Alice Bailey describes the emotional level as humanity's battlefield. Feelings, sensations, drives and reactions forcefully drive into the human landscape. The problem is that people don't know how valuable they are and how best to use them.

Emotions as we experience them are unique to humanity. We are envied for it by beings from other dimensions. It is also claimed that some of these predators feed on our negative emotions. Does that feel plausible? Watch the news day in, day out!

Feelings as well as thoughts radiate frequencies. Read the book by Dr. medical dr phil. David R. Hawkins to research the subject thoroughly and most informatively. He classifies emotional vibrations from positive to negative. Man has received the great gift of being able to choose and make decisions. This is not only a gift, but also an extremely powerful opportunity for growth through the exercise of free will. Most of the time he is hardly aware of it.

Emotions and feelings are part of an excellent feedback system. They show you non-stop how much you are in tune with your highest authority or not. Are you one with yourself, is there contentment, clarity and well-being in you? If the connection to the soul is impaired, you deal with restlessness, resentment, rage, anger and neurotic tendencies. They arise from inner friction, from conflicts and distortions towards the inner being. Every emotional location determination provides clear feedback. It's that easy. But humans tend to distort emotions, misinterpret them and suppress them. It may work for a short time. In the long run, this strategy causes disharmonies in the body, in the psyche and in the daily routine, eg as a cause of accidents, misfortune, entanglements as well as confusion and unfavorable coincidences.

Before we go any further, we must develop the courage to face and accept our emotions. Even if they don't flatter us. Truth consists in confronting what is. The personal situation is no worse or better than other people: please do not compare or talk around it, and create excuses, reasons or lies. It is the way it is: if we can do something with this principle, we open the door to liberating energetic processes. Yes, the truth sets you free. But there is more: we discover the possibility of transforming the distressing feelings - either by transforming them or by increasing their frequency.

Quantum physics states that everything is energy. Thus, we direct our focus on the emotional energy mass from a higher perspective, from a general, comprehensive point of view. At the same time, visualizing the center of the disco ball is helpful to gain an overview of the emotional state. The first effect is that we are less involved and things take on a more abstract or schematic character. The distance gained gives us more clarity, distance, objectivity and a fair view of the topic. These are encouraging assumptions. At the same time, harmful reactions such as fear, shame, and guilt are largely alleviated before dissipating entirely. So we come to the transformation.

EXERCISE A: TRANSFORMATION OF NEGATIVITY

A negative emotion often feels dark, solid, hard, heavy, or overwhelming. The first thing we do is to loosen these qualities. For this we move our hands in the air just in front of us where we imagine the chosen emotional energy. And this with the intention of making the heaviness a little lighter. The dark becomes lighter, the solid more supple, the hardness softens, the heaviness becomes lighter and the oppressive becomes fluffier. Yes, fluffier: there is no better description for this energy transformation. Everyone instinctively knows how that feels: this is an important and meaningful step for us. Namely that subjective approach that knows immediately what is and how it feels. Gradually and with breaks we loosen and soothe the compact sensations so that we can deal with them better. First, they don't seem so threatening anymore. Second, this technique ensures that we don't get stuck in the maelstrom.

Often the situation will no longer seem so important, maybe even a little ridiculous - if we can still muster up a little humor. This enables us to initiate better solutions, actions and changes. We have more power for the learning task or for the nurturing and positive aspects of the situation.

The transformation work may be repeated several times until the blockage is resolved or until it no longer affects us. It is best if we allow ourselves breaks from time to time in order to gradually integrate our progress.

EXERCISE B: INCREASE THE FREQUENCY

The second method is less emotional but more characterized by concepts and intellect. Sensing the energetic shift is still important. The art of self-observation is used here to track when the emotional state is falling: heavy, depressed mood, upset, anger and other low emotions. Under no circumstances should you remain in the unfavorable vibration for a long time after you have recognized and named it. Noticing and interpreting it are essential because it acts as feedback as explained above. The part of you that is watching the sensation takes over instead of being at the mercy of emotional chaos. The inner observer is able to formulate the emotion precisely. The exact expression comes from courage, clarity and honesty towards oneself. Even if it hurts for a moment. This is just a brief reaction of the ego that has to admit the truth. But self-observation is quickly rewarded. Because soon there is a relief in the intensity of the negative feeling. But that's just the beginning. Because you now have the opportunity to choose a lighter, brighter, more positive emotion. We are not expecting that all is well and done at once. Nevertheless, you are able to achieve a situation which is gradually improving. Well done! A smile may also help, because humor is like a lubricant: where there is a traffic jam, laughing or even a smile brings a little gentleness and flow. Experience this moment very consciously and be thankful for the healing miracles that you are currently causing. This shift supports your self-determination and in turn influences your self-esteem and your sense of self-responsibility. And the immediate reward is contentment, relaxation, and general well-being.

We will learn more methods in our workshop: "Activate your inner healer ".

CONCLUSION: Based on what has been examined here, it is evident that the activation of the inner healer on the emotional level consists in stabilizing one's own mood, the basic coloring of the emotional level and maintaining fluctuations within a certain balance. This means that an optimistic, confident outlook on life is consciously cultivated, like a beautiful garden that produces healthy and strong plants that delight the heart over and over again. At the same time, one can imagine the garden inside, which has a nourishing, inspiring and solution-oriented effect if one makes oneself receptive to the inherent security and stillness. This targeted and constantly cultivated balance acts as medicine, as an immune booster, as a soothing light source in the cells and in the aura. Without a certain emotional stability, psychoimmunology suffers in the long run.

PART 4: HEAD CINEMA AND MENTAL

Beliefs and misconceptions
Clarity, will and intention
Psychoimmunology
Heart and brain

We produce thoughts all day long - non-stop, so to speak. Except when we're meditating or daydreaming. Now it is a matter of observing and sorting out the quality of our thoughts.

Our mental activity and our emotional world are very closely coordinated. The first directly influences the second, although sometimes it is difficult for us to distinguish which comes first, for the two are closely intertwined. Therefore, it is not always self-evident to identify and objectify the key idea. It may be that the mental image is so buried in the psyche that it is "overlooked". The belief "It's always like this" can make life hell through unconscious programming. The observer shapes reality through his mental/ emotional orientation: if this is friendly and constructive, it will positively shape the experiences and their interpretation. For example, you will want to highlight the benefit or good points of the situation and learn something from it. Or you will strive to make the best of it and grow through it and be thankful for the experiences. This attitude creates a worthwhile, meaningful life. From this perspective, one is happy to be alive and finds being enjoyable as a human in human community. Conversely, you can create hell on earth for yourself and others. It's our choice. The exercise of free will is the engine of soul development within the earthly incarnation. It expresses itself through personal, mental focus and can create a humane world in harmony with nature, with other kingdoms of nature (the animal, plant and mineral kingdoms) and with the earth.

Head cinema with recurring thoughts, thought carousel with the playing of negative scenarios in the imagination, as well as letting illogical and untidy trains of thought run, form a confused energy around the head, which is directly transferred to the emotional level. Feeling-Thinking is one. This powerful combination affects the physical condition and physiology in different ways. Mostly unconscious and immediate. Here are some physiological functions related to mental health.

The nervous system: the electrical impulses of the nerves are transmitted via the neurovegetative system to muscles and organs, because we are electrical beings.

The endocrine system: it is responsible for glands and hormones as well as for the complex interaction of the organs. Of course, also for the mood: cheerful with endorphins, combative thanks to adrenaline, full of relish with estrogen and testosterone, ready for sleep with melatonin - to provide simple examples.

The immune system: it masters the fight against infections, but it also shapes psychological resistance in the form of regeneration potential and resilience.

The interplay between the mental processes and the physical state of the facial expression and facial expressions to the physical posture as for example is taught in physiognomy or in psychosomatics. Or also in the insights of the Schüßler salt face therapy.

The environment I create and interact with. From this it becomes dream life or a vicious circle.

This brief description of processes may provide insights into the mechanisms of one's own life. If we want to reach deeper into the ethereal world, the aura together with the chakras actually surpass the physiological phenomena. The physical is the visible end product of the subtle influences, the invisible, such as vibration, thought and emotion.

Becoming more conscious means insight and knowledge and directing the intention to the main goal, to the essential or even to the basic principles and values behind the motivation and life drive. This includes the will and willingness to take the reins and shape your own world better or differently. The intention is to consciously direct attention to the desired outcome in a creative way. It is taken for granted that the goal has been achieved – without a doubt. With a little practice, it can develop into an artistic pleasure and thus create something fulfilling and new.

The heart and brain together form a relatively newly discovered combination, research into which dates back to the early 1990s. New for science - but not for mysticism or for subtle perception.

Forty thousand cells in the heart have been identified that resemble brain cells. However, they are in the heart and thereby form the heart intelligence. Unlike the brain, the heart is one in its sentience: these special neurons, called neurites, have holistic perception as opposed to the head or reason. The brain is divided into two hemispheres and the mind is polar in orientation: it oscillates between so-called positive and negative and other polar terms: favorable-unfavorable, warm-cold, early-late etc. The heart chakra relates to the Unity and represents the center of truth. Gregg Bradon did a great job spreading this discovery and its consequences.

EXERCISE A:

The heart knows what is harmonious and authentic. The heart donates the wisdom of the heart and opens the way to unified intelligence. Harmony with the soul is either there or not: that is the individual truth. It's not a "two-way affair." To gain this holistic wisdom, it is enough to calm down and put your hand on your heart. The divided, vacillating aspect (ego, mind, reason, head-heaviness) gradually calms down, allowing the heart intelligence to step forward and express itself. Again, she is free from ego-splitting: "Yes, but...", doubt, manipulation, influence and other confusion or weakening of intent. As you place your hand on your heart, you achieve a state of oneness and alignment with your inner being. This is how you recognize what is coherent and authentic. This is how people discover who they are and what they want – from the heart.

PART 5: THE INNER DIVINE AND ACCORDANCE WITH ESSENCE

Responsibility for self: free from ego and expectation
Spirituality and mysticism: free, immortal and limitless.
Trust and grace
Faith and Immediate Knowledge: Intuition, Inspiration and Higher Guidance.

Now we have reached the higher chakras, the spiritual dimensions and layers of the aura. There is the question of the meaning of existence and in particular of the present incarnation. Either there is a friendly worldview in which people feel carried and nourished by a higher power and are surrounded by benevolent beings. The human being is embedded in the big picture, capable of learning and being creative. Thus he contributes to the highest good and is in contact with him at eye level in the vertical connection between heaven and earth and in the horizontal communication with his environment. This earthling is grateful for life, optimistic and confident. Because of his healthy attitude, he attracts positive events or situations from which he is able to highlight uplifting aspects and learn from them. He feels good in his soul. His development is in line with his soul destiny.

Or vice versa, the view is rather hostile, pessimistic and hopeless. The pessimistic worldview shapes the experiences that are gained. A person who cultivates this negatively colored view tends to be anxious sometimes to the point of paranoia and encounters uncomfortable people and situations in life. By concentrating on negative experiences and their course, by terrible scripts and programming that plays out in the head from morning to night, this unfavorably shaped worldview acts like a magnet for unfavorable, pathogenic and hopeless relationships and coincidences. Your immune system and your entire defenses such as resilience, regenerative capacity and processing of experiences are impaired and perhaps reduced. She likes to hold on to her injuries, to being offended, to her role as a victim. She faces many things with fear, she has the impression that she should constantly protect herself and always expects the worst. When it does, her ego is proud that she was "right." "I told you so", "I knew it". Their tunnel vision and pessimistic expectations color and distort everything so that life becomes a vale of suffering. A series of mishaps unfold in her life and her adoration of suffering continues with the fatalistic conviction: "That's life".

On the inner healer, these two opposing attitudes have either a beneficial or a braking effect. The doomsayer will even deny his own regenerative power or "don't believe in it". His view of the future is sad and set for failure. His mental expectations shape his reality with restlessness, revulsion, reticence, stubborn, negative beliefs such as "It was always like that", "It's just like that" and rejection of the truth. What is observed is influenced by the observer and his expectations. This in turn attracts experiences to which he directs his mental and emotional charge. The result is the mirror of his beliefs, his unconscious fears and his other negative inner images. As we have learned, the combination of thoughts and emotions forms a direct unit that shapes and shapes the physique. This influence on the cells corresponds to the process of somatization within psychosomatics. In this way, the susceptibility to illness increases and the ability to recover becomes weaker.

The terrain is built and prepared by these backgrounds: that's why I went into detail about these contrasting attitudes. The milieu resonates: either with an affected organism or it promotes a powerful immune response with a milder course. Viruses, bacteria, fungi and other parasites as well as the microbiome find either an acidic (disease-promoting) or an alkaline soil (health-promoting) in the body. The great Antoine Béchamp - chemist, doctor and pharmacist 1816 - 1908 - scientifically examined the milieu and with his knowledge saved many people from fatal diseases.

Actually, the laws are easy to understand.

Their implementation represents a lifelong, natural work in itself, involving all levels: body, emotions, psyche, spirit, energetics and the environment (fellow human beings and the so-called reality with the events that are part of our lives).

In a broader sense, we can perhaps define the milieu as the result of our disposition and what we make of it: an interaction between genetics and epigenetics, what we bring with us and consciously aspired developments, and an interface between our own universe and its resonance with the environment. The "terrain" is another term for it. It acts like a magnet and resonates with events that are at similar frequencies. When it is right, there is agreement between the inner and outer world. So you feel good on all levels and you are fulfilled. Because your life is how it should be. These are the people who are said to have "nothing to talk about," or have nothing to complain about.

In order to reach this state, you will work on your issues. You will discover that you are the most important person in your life. Yes, your well-being, meeting your priorities, and nurturing your lifestyle by always being true to yourself are part of the key. Only then can you really help others without wasting your strength or depriving your fellow human beings of their strength. You may be so centered and at peace that you need to do or say little to have a positive impact on those around you. Your energetic charisma is transferred to your environment and interacts with it through your perception.

If everyone cared about raising their own vibration, we would experience a huge transformation of humanity in no time. People would not have time to meddle in the private affairs of others. The frequency change would actually make itself felt in a short time. Less fighting and more compassion could be translated into solidarity, consideration, helping, participating, friendship, heart quality, joy, healing, insights, balance, peace, etc. Because your own charisma is more harmonious, your light-filled contribution shines out into the world. It couldn't be easier: it doesn't cost any energy, no money, no politics, no rules. Just your conscious alignment with your inner unity. Because you are an aspect of the universal whole, you find your place in the great puzzle. The more people cultivate their personal vibration, the easier man recognizes his task. Each time we open a door of consciousness, we prepare the way for those to come.

Even as a child I admired this ingenious simplicity. In this way, the divine clarity reverses the polarity of the ego and the negative forces, because they no longer receive any nourishment in the form of fixation as well as distorted and burdened energies and emotions. For the sole reason that everyone is getting better. Eventually, people will be able to shed their recurring trauma and confront their true potential. Imagine that more and more people - starting with themselves - would set themselves this goal!

In addition, all peaceful, natural, nourishing and healthy wavelengths are beginning to converge, having an exponential impact on the well-being of humanity and all other beings on Earth and other planets. Other beings in the cosmos are also welcoming this increase in vibration. Thus, each of us can contribute to the greater whole by dedicating ourselves to being in tune with our higher authority. It does not rule out that we also courageously go outside and actively represent our concerns there. On the contrary, it is part of it: both methods of expression complement each other - from the inside out.

But the beginning is up to you: You with yourself - in internalization. If you are then ready to appear outwardly with equal vibrations, the optimal situation has been reached. Both for you and for the others. And when you stay in that space, where everyone is true to themselves, yet resonates with and enriches the community, a mature and quality social exchange emerges.

Again and again we can remind ourselves of our essence. To the inherent freedom of the soul, to our immortal and limitless part of being. Because that's exactly what we are at the core. In fact, if man is able to identify with his origin, he is the only entity that has the conscious ability to transmute and increase energy. We are everyday alchemists when we wake up to our true essence.

Instead of judging and negatively burdening yourself, others and events, you would direct your focus to what is important and to their basic motivation. Rather than wasting your energy and distracting yourself with superficial, irrelevant details, you would immediately attain a higher level of consciousness through your spiritual focus. This increases your mental and general strength and at the same time you open up beneficial, human and harmonious solutions and changes in all areas. First, one must be able to see the good side or inherent potential in any situation. Sometimes it is necessary to tame the first negative or fearful reaction in order to take a particularly creative look at the current situation. Which - frankly - is not always obvious.

Another consequence of this attitude is the strengthening of discernment, along with agency. Thus we motivate our inner observer to keep his focus on the beneficial and the wise.

Basic trust is the basis of all interactions. i.e. we are constantly being challenged by the universe to give an advance of confidence as a basic attitude in every human exchange, as well as in our relationship with the higher authority. This has to do with the basic attitude: friendly or hostile view of life as explained above. Pretty easy, isn't it? The consequence: the basic trust is neither fixed on the self nor on the exact, short-term result. On the contrary: it is generous, open and lives in the knowledge that we get what is due to us, that the possibilities are countless and that everything is as it should be under the given circumstances. No, it is not fatalism, but being able to see through the fact that larger connections are at work according to the law of resonance. Thus, the rules of the game are relatively simple, even if they can always pose a challenge. Then we live in the present and let the energy flow where it is drawn to by the resonation. When there is optimal resonance, we receive grace and happiness, with everything being right: in the right place at the right time, with the right people.

Belief is the glue that combines trust along with purposeful expectation. Faith is the catalyst that puts the parts of one's own worldview together: Providence and leadership are expressed through intuitive ideas and feelings, through the inner voice, through meaningful coincidences. To do this, you have to listen, calm down a little, observe quietly and then act consistently with enthusiasm. Try simple, everyday things to start with. Over time, you can refine these principles and incorporate them into more complex decisions.

CONCLUSION: The spiritual, mental perception of the self and its place in the big picture transfers directly to the other levels: mental/psychic, energetic, emotional/emotional as well as the physical layers, which in turn is reflected by the environment and by the events. Think about what connection you maintain to your individual soul and to your higher authority (everything that is). In other words, this relationship with the divine part is our most intimate relationship. You play with your senses, body, feelings and thoughts on the earthly stage for several decades in order to contribute your personal expression to the big picture. How do you want to shape your life story so that it is worth living and at the same time becomes an honorable obolus to the world soul? For example: a long, good life as it should be (in tune with your true self) and where everything you need is present?

EXERCISE A:

The self-responsibility and the individuation process are so advanced at this stage that it is no longer suitable to make suggestions. However, I would recommend you to pick 1 or 2 terms from the last 2 paragraphs and keep them in mind throughout the day. E.g., faith, trust, catalyst, world view, leadership, providence etc. What does this word mean to you?

how do you live it How do you express it in your life? E.g. your trust. What is your worldview now? What did it look like before?

One step higher: You take this term with you into the meditation and look at its meanings and what you connect it with (associations) in a seed meditation.

You can complete the exercise by applying the selected vocabulary in one of the different dimensions on the material or emotional or spiritual level. What would your faith be like in the material world? How is your trust expressed in the emotional realm? In a spiritual sense?

Feel free to develop your own individual variations of this exercise. They will serve you well.

Part 6: ENERGY

Empirical values and basic principles
Individuality: resonance and incompatibility
I am my personal expert
Self-help and self-test: energetic methods and dowsing

I can't omit the energetics, because they complement the 4 levels mentioned in a pictorial and lived way. Feeling/thinking and imagination direct the flow of energy to the desired state - internally but also in everyday life. The inner guidance or the uplifting, creative quality and the truthful are the fuel. The opposite is characterized by debilitating blocks, confusion and deception, and elements that are destabilizing or unsettling.

EXERCISE A:

What is predominant in your life right now? Examine your relationship to the divine within or your thought processes. What are you broadcasting in general? What are you radiating out into the world? You are also welcome to follow the energy in reverse: from the physical to the spiritual. The physical and emotional condition as well as the living conditions reflect the inner order or disorder.

What proportions are they divided into in your everyday life? How much order is there in your existence? Not according to external standards, but through your immediate sensation: I feel good in my life, in my body, in my soul and in my spirit because I know what reality I want to create and what I attract. Can you affirm yourself when you look yourself in the mirror? Can you hold your gaze for a moment? Is your conscience clear and right for you? Then you have achieved contentment, which indicates a high frequency. I congratulate you and thank you for your harmonious contribution to the whole.

If it isn't, be glad that the confusion or discrepancy shows you where harmonization is still needed. Take that as momentary guidance and be thankful for it. It helps you and the universe to achieve greater balance. But relax, because the game is always on, so there's no pressure, just flow in the right direction, bringing you back into line again and again. Until the harmonious moments get longer and longer and the disharmony practically disappears. Then you can say: I am one with myself.

When alignment with your true self is your yardstick, alignment gradually becomes more stable and part of your normal life. Everything else depends on it. But you're still responsible for maintaining that high aspiration or you'll lose momentum. This means that you keep the frequency as high as possible. There is no general recipe, because the individual impetus comes from within. You have your personal values and basic principles: they show you your own path in accordance with your conscience and your own values.

Of course, moral and ethical decisions are not made overnight. They represent a great responsibility: all the more so because they are challenged by distraction, authoritarianism, deception, superficiality, fear-inducing measures and narratives, and insecurity. What is right for me? Man is so alienated from himself that he no longer knows or feels it - and tries to avoid responsibility. The result is compliance, obedience, cowardice, running along. Sooner or later – no matter how good the excuses sound – inner conflicts arise. In the long run, the inner split becomes unbearable. You choose between: "I stand by myself", "I am one with myself", "I have a clear conscience" or "I am torn", "I cannot look myself in the eye" along with the consequences such as ignorance, Repressing, hiding, shame and guilt issues.

is right, appropriate, healthy, uplifting for oneself. For example: "I know that this natural remedy always helps me in this situation". The resonance or - on the contrary - the incompatibility is noticeable or even measurable. Journaling can be helpful. It may be that the results are outdated over time, so it is important to be adaptable: my body reacts differently than 20 years ago, my soul needs something different, my spirit always wants to discover something new. People like to recommend all kinds of things. However, if my system does not resonate with the solution offered, with the home remedy or with the prescription, the well -intentioned suggestion is ineffective and could even be harmful.

For this I have worked out and compiled a number of methods from traditional tried practices or from little-known sources. The knowledge is best passed on in private lessons. It can also be done in a small group, depending on how profound or spiritual the goal and the desired level are. These learning units are individually adapted and include intuitive, energetic and / or radiesthetic (pendulum or tensor) work but also practical exercises with the strength of the hands and fingers. Thus we have reliable techniques to achieve energetic results in all private areas. These are "aids for self-help" to come to terms with your own soul. Once internalized, they are available to you anytime, anywhere. Together with the inner healer we develop precise protocols and methodological procedures that are easy to learn but require regular practice.

In this way we become individual, own guides and healers. We exercise self-responsibility and practice the knowledge that comes from within and is implemented for oneself. Because nobody knows better about me than I do. Freedom is determined by one's own independence and self-determination. I am my own expert. Only my higher authority stands above me: it is my benchmark, my lighthouse, but also my monitor and compass. And not just from a vague intuition, but from the innermost true core. Each individual's path to finding himself or being in harmony with himself is a purely individual matter for which everyone is responsible.

When we leave our body at the end of this incarnation and weigh its contents, we gain insight into the whole process including our motivations and priorities. It's no use saying, "Everyone did or said that," "They wanted me to behave like this, do that...", etc. You may have to face the fact that you often lose your responsibility and discernment gave to others. You have allowed this or empowered others to interfere in your unfolding. This speaks against your integrity and the self-determination of your soul.

People often forget that their life is a very special gift and that it is about living this existence with mindfulness and responsibility. Man allows himself to be misled by distractions (superficiality, overindulgence, news, lies and superstition) but also by certain substances (pharmaceutical and other drugs, food, contaminated water, unhealthy habits, illusions) away from his true path.

Instead of using his immediate feeling, intuition and discernment, he lets himself be done with anything. Sloane Bella, an eminent American medium, claims there is a spiritual war going on - and she's right. She knows what she's talking about because she has an extraordinarily strong and reliable perception of the invisible. We have everything it takes to discern the truc from the false through inner listening, inspiration, gut feeling and intelligence. Entities intent on the suffering of humanity operate in secret. They deceive and manipulate, creating fear, confusion and insecurity. It is therefore essential to sharpen and exercise one's own perception. It is up to us to stimulate, develop and nurture these skills. Because we've sunk into a comfortable, hypnotic stupor. This is where humanity's greatest chance lies: to finally become human. Inevitably, however, she will awaken to her inner divinity, live it out and implement it in everyday life. The process unfolds. He is under the highest light, for on this depends the future of humanity on earth and its place among other cosmic peoples. The healing, the renewal on a grand scale is on its way, on all levels of the being. It is in our own hands and, above all, our responsibility. The divine human is about to give birth to himself under the guidance and security of the whole universe.

How we think of and about ourselves, how we look at ourselves, sets out the starting point of our place, our contribution, our evolution in the great divine puzzle. As a divine being, I know that I have everything I need within me. When I know who I am and perceive myself as an infinite and immortal entity, I flow with the flow of my life: I live my life, not other people's. When I am convinced that everything is going well for me, I am confident and also attract solutions and opportunities that bring harbingers of fulfilling development. Now it is essential to include the notion of process: things unfold constantly and little by little, gradually, not in a flash. Even if something seems to happen suddenly, previous events and contexts are also to be included. The so-called reality is only the end product or the visible result of inner processes, hidden or unfolding on other planes (the astral world). Everything flows into each other and with each other in a huge cosmic dance.

in the universal framework: there are numerous possibilities and no definitive variant has yet been determined. Because this depends on YOU. Not only from you, but from all individual beings who carry light within them. And above all, how and how much they make their own luminosity shine. Basically everything that is alive carries light within it, and IS light in and of itself. You see, you're never alone.

Therefore, you can always concentrate on what is alive, on what is healthy: on a small scale, in your microcosm, and on a large scale, in the macrocosm. Processes are subject to their own rhythms and move up and down and back and forth: sometimes good, sometimes bad, depending on how we evaluate and feel the movement. Instead of getting stuck in the lower curve, let the current carry you further up and welcome the big wave - starting now. That is devotion. Surrender is only possible when you trust the flow that you have internalized as a necessary change that conforms to the laws of evolution. Frankly, it is necessary to adopt a higher viewpoint, a more mature point of view. It involves the ability in the here and now to make the appropriate, current move, and not necessarily aim for immediate gratification of your needs and ego. This is the exercise that repeatedly gives you deep fulfillment and coherently shapes your career. The healthy outweighs the pathological: the former is always present wherever life pulsates and trembles. Even the smallest amount is enough: as soon as the gaze, the attention is directed to the existing hopeful potential, the vibration increases. The human/the situation/the development then vibrates at an increasing frequency. From this point on, healing is stimulated, regeneration and evolution initiated. A lot of energy is produced to find and maintain balance again.

It would be good if medicine would take this principle to heart, if people would direct their attention to what is alive, hopeful and wholesome. I get what I expect. We promote this not only in the head and through nice talk, but also from the depths of the being to the superconscious.

Defining and setting your expectations for you as part of humanity is self-empowering (empowering), liberating and quite beneficial. All sensations are strengthened: hormones (endorphins, serotonin) are released, which in turn make you happy and confident. Confidence and positive perceptions and expectations of those around us will bring out the best in them. We can handle the few disappointments. We don't always fulfill the wishes of others either. The focus on the highest principles and the evolution of the soul gives us the drive for our actions, our motivations and for the harmony that arises from them.

Conclusion: The spiritual aspect is the greatest force that influences everything else. When completely denied, one finds it difficult to achieve the inner serenity necessary for balance and contentment. Even if the light penetrates all levels, each layer of the organism is responsible for its own balance. The physical order (health) reflects the order in the cosmos, feelings are an expression of consciousness and thoughts are the spark ray from the spirit through to the reality that we create and experience every day. What we surround ourselves with is the result and mirror of our relationship with the eternal and inextinguishable divine presence within. Whether we know it or not.

PART 7: FINDINGS AND INSIGHTS

Now we have first gone through the physical body through to the mind. In reality, however, the subtle, the intention of the soul, arises first. In the incarnated state, the invisible is the part that determines our development and well-being. This in turn happens through thoughts (also unconscious ones) and through our attitude to life, as well as through dealing with our health and our interaction with our environment.

Life is sacred. No institution or dogma is required to come to this realization. Just observation and a little self-respect along with mindfulness and a willingness to nurture what was born. In the hope that this booklet will be easier to read, I have deliberately not covered the deeper and more hidden connections. It is meant as a practical impulse so that the individual encounters his or her nature with more mindfulness and appreciation. Health, natural beauty, happiness, good self-esteem, a clear head, a sharp intellect, love and respect for yourself and those around you are gifts of existence. We have become too accustomed to undignified circumstances - less so in rich countries, but materialism prevails there and some tend to their possessions more than their mind, emotions or body. You leave that to the psychiatrist, the psychologist and the doctor. Medicine and all healing professions are essential because humanity is so traumatized and disconnected from its spiritual connection that it will continue to need its services. Also, to some degree, sickness is a part of our experience. Harmonization, treatment and care are there to bring us back into balance. Wouldn't it be wiser to acknowledge the natural regenerative powers and include them in the healing process? To interact with these tremendous forces of self-renewal by knowing the individual reactions better and always first using methods that stimulate and support the self-regenerative potential such as acupuncture, homeopathy, massage, radionics and others. Of course, medicine will also play its part, but not to shoot at sparrows with cannons, because after that it's really difficult to mend the sparrows, isn't it? Then they get the diagnosis: "incurable"!

The physical body as well as the other different levels of the human being, like everything else in nature, are self-regenerating: why can trees live 150 years in undisturbed places? Why does nature take over the entire environment again in such a short time if it follows its course unhindered and freely? Every cell in our body is constantly renewing itself. The mind is also capable of processing and integrating processes in order to attain maturity and wisdom.

Most people have been taught, directly or indirectly, that they are unimportant, too inconspicuous, too stupid, or somehow incapable of really making a difference in this world. However, the universe is calling, "What do you want to experience? What do you, unique being, have to contribute? Show who you are! do you know who you are You are an expression of unity." The universe wants – through you – to become more and more aware of itself – just like you and for this it created you. In return, you constantly receive new powers as long as you are alive. This is the most fascinating journey of your life: your self-discovery leads you to the secrets of your splendor, your power and your self-healing with the help of your inner healer. This in turn is part of your connection with infinity and eternity. From there you come and there you will continue your way. Like all other living entities. And as a result, not only are all human beings equal with each other, but also with all other living beings, from animals to plants, to minerals and to planet earth.

Harmony with one's own core promotes access to the inner healer. She/he will help you to identify and care for your needs. She/he promotes inner communication to your different parts. In addition, she / he is responsible for the coordination between them. You can now receive the wisdom of your body, your psyche, your higher self in order to interact with them. They empower you to radiate your true light into the world. They empower you to fulfill your soul destiny and take your place in the greater whole.

Your inner healer also helps you attract or choose the healing modalities and helpful therapists. Above all, however, it is the inner healer, the inner aspect that helps you to become and remain whole, whole and authentic. Because health on all levels corresponds to our natural, original state.

THREE - DAY SEMINAR TO ACTIVATE THE INNER HEALER

DAY ONE

The different levels of our existence: we go through them in detail as a helpful and concrete model
The visible and the invisible part?
What is balance? How do I get balance? How do I maintain the harmonious state?
The subject of trust, basic trust, trust in the processes of life, self-confidence
What is health? Does health have to be expensive?
We respond to individual interests and needs.

DAY TWO

Codex Humanus, the book of humanity: THE taboo-free standard work of naturopathy
Brief introduction and individual advice
Inner communication to activate the inner healing power and for recovery
Classification of harmonization methods: from thoughts to allopathy
What is helpful for me? What do I need?
Overview of test methods

DAY THREE

Practice day
Group work and individual exercises on test methods
Various working documents.
Get reliable results
Competence and Limits
Self-responsibility, discernment and decision-making ability
Helping others and respect for free will/ethics
Healthy and free

Bibliography

Aurélienne Dauguet

Guide to your cosmic energies

Aura discovery

Published in German language only.

ISBN 978-3-944700-02-1 (Paperback)

ISBN 978-3-944700-12-0 (e-book)

Everything that is alive possesses an aura.

To perceive energies and subtle emanations is part of the natural talents of living beings. Rediscovering this opens up a fresh, new look at everyday life and broadens horizons.

The book "Travel Guide to your Cosmic Energies - Aura Discovery" takes the reader on a journey of discovery into the various levels and dimensions of the human aura.

It contains both theoretical treatises on the different layers of the aura, such as the etheric body, the emotional body or the mental body, as well as practical exercises for the correct handling of the aura.

Aurélienne Dauguet

AURATHERAPY

for DOCTORS, THERAPISTS

and interested laymen

Published in German language only.

ISBN 978-3-944700-42-7 (Paperback)

ISBN 978-3-944700-72-4 (e-book)

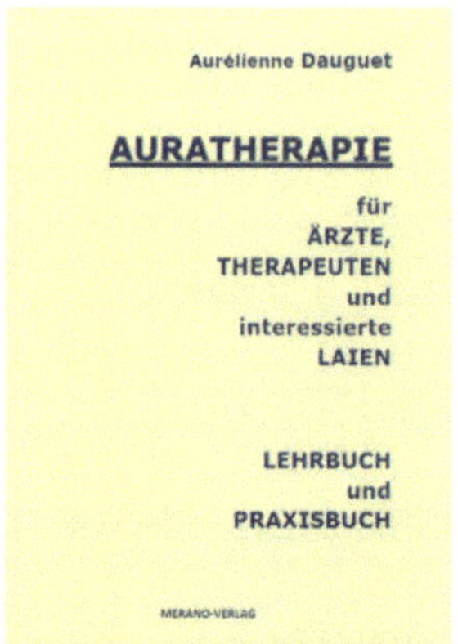

This book consists of two parts:

In this textbook, the focus is on the theoretical background, on the aura and its different subtle layers. Energetic approaches to the subtle anatomy are considered. The various aura pathologies and their straightening are treated in detail. The clairvoyant access to the past and future, to incarnational experiences, to prophylactic aura care and to aura surgery are presented and integrated into the therapeutic framework.

This useful book contains practice-oriented exercises that train the therapist's subtle perceptions, and techniques that maintain, protect, clarify, harmonize and treat the aura and its subtle dimensions. It also contains testimonials that support the theory and implementation of aura therapy, as well as inventions by the author.

Only available in German.

Aurélienne Dauguet

LIGHT-NUTRITION

MY NEW LIFE AS A BREATHARIAN

ISBN: 978-3-944700-18-2 (paperback)

ISBN: 978-3-944700-28-1 (e-book)

This is the author's account of her light nourishment process. She describes how she managed to switch from "normal" food to photon nourishment. This report underlines the transformations during the first year of her new life with light nourishment.

This description is authentic, down to earth, clear and simple.

The purpose of her contribution is to facilitate the understanding and spiritual access to light nourishment in a human and realistic way.

In no way is this book an encouragement to practice breatharianism. This process is a purely internal one and can only be a call from the soul. There is nothing to prove and no one to convince.

For the author, the choice to convert into the Prana mode was one of the deepest most relevant in her life, along with the freedom to stop or continue the light nourishment at any time.

Aurélienne Dauguet

CREATING A NEW SELF-IMAGE

ISBN: 978-3-944700-24-3 (Paperback)

ISBN: 978-3-944700-34-2 (e-book)

Am I just the way I am and always have been and there is nothing to be changed about? Am I also there on earth to discover, explore, develop and express myself and my being? Or am I incarnated here to refine and ennoble my personality and to connect it in alignment with my essence?

I progress into the world, self-determined and authentic, remembering my inherent divine spark. As a creator and in harmony with my higher self, I express my eternal and multidimensional aspects in everyday life.

This encouraging manual about self-knowledge throws a transformative light on the humans as spiritual beings embedded within the current phase of upheaval and breakthrough. The metamorphosis is in full swing. The necessity and the responsibility to create an upgrade of our humanness lies in the hands of each individual. A new personal self-image directly creates and contributes to a differentiated identity of the entire humanity.

Aurélienne Dauguet

The Conman

or

Of loving and dying

ISBN: 978-3-944700-29-8 (paperback)

ISBN: 978-3-944700-89-2 (e-book)

This true story gives amazing insights into karmic contexts and old beliefs that display outdated behavior.

Unexpected connections prevail and are revealed during this exceptional journey to Normandy in the purpose of meeting with a respected author.

Similar to the unfolding of the images of a kaleidoscope, different fates unfold from ancient Egypt to a liberating future full of luminous promises. Rich in insights which confront unacceptable traditional and relationships patterns, the spotlight of consciousness shines on them, in order to transform and heal them.

Reflections and mental abilities underpin every day of the stay in northern France. Eternally valid principles stand out from the entertaining story and lend us a deeper understanding of one's own life, including the processes of loving and dying.

Aurélienne Dauguet

SETTING HEALTHY BOUNDARIES

ISBN: 978-3-944700-22-9 (paperback)

ISBN: 978-3-944700-92-2 (e-book)

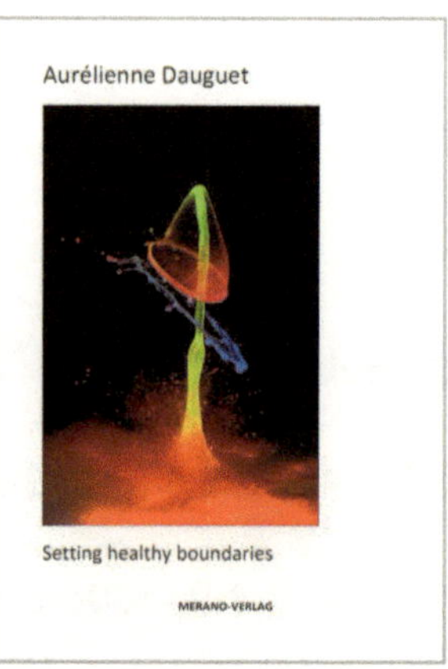

Consideration, goodwill and respect for the space and the free will of our fellow humans is part and parcel of the interaction between people of the new era.

Not only between persons but also within our own unity as individual, we practice mindfulness towards our physical body, our emotional aspects, our cognitive abilities as well as towards the spiritual dimensions of our very being.

In her 12th book (comprising the complete publications in German, French and English), Aurélienne Dauguet deals with the profound topic of building up healthy boundaries on all levels of our individual beingness and also within the collective realms of life.

Politeness, goodwill, and a humanist approach are indispensable. Ethical consequences are attached to our relationships. It is a duty to encounter conscious life with appreciation. On the other hand, any infringement upon the development of other human beings definitely represents one of the heaviest karmic burden possible.

About the author

Aurélienne Dauguet (born in Paris in 1953) has a pronounced subtle perception ability since her youth.

Initially working as a nurse (additional psychiatry), she is now a lecturer at the Paracelsus Schools in Germany and Switzerland for aura therapy, subtle radionics, the dying process from a holistic perspective, spiritual healing, etc.

The current range of courses is available from the Paracelsus schools.

Further training: Lithotherapy, aura work, aromatherapy, flower and precious stone essences dowsing, subtle radionics (without device), "Radionic Practitioner" after the "British Radionic Association" and with David Tansley, Aura Soma Training with Vicky Wall. Aurélienne Dauguet was an Aura Soma teacher.

The teaching and seminar activities on the subject of aura take place throughout Europe.

For about 30 years she has been offering reading and cleaning of the aura, psychic writing, individual sessions, one-to-one lessons and remote support in German, English and French, both in her own rooms and by telephone.

If interested, see contact information.

Contact:
Aurélienne Dauguet
Schiessgrabenstraße 28

86150 Augsburg
Tel: 0049 821 / 45 40 77 44

WEBSITE: aureliennedauguet.com